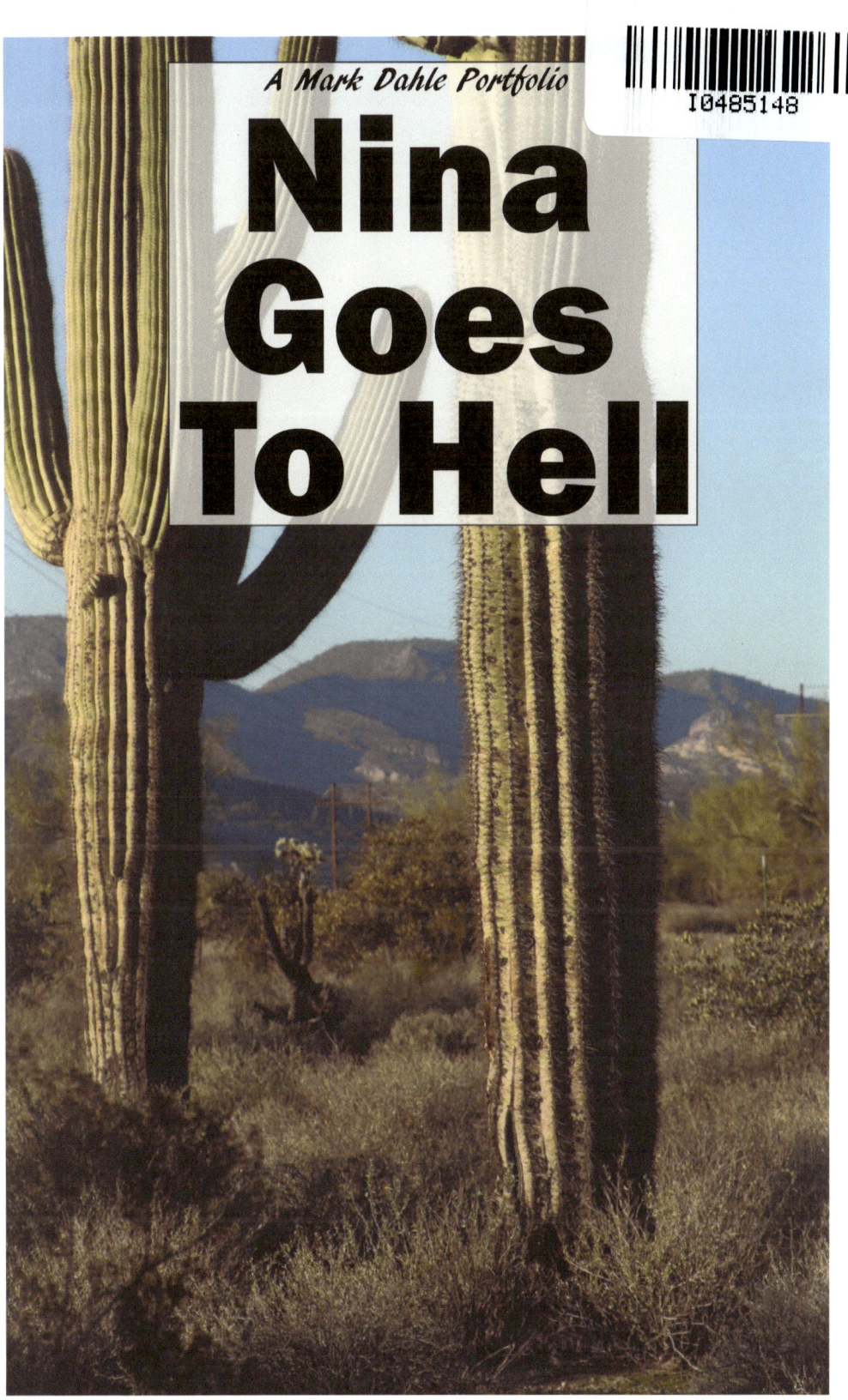

A Mark Dahle Portfolio

Nina Goes To Hell

Mark Dahle Portfolios can be read in a few minutes and enjoyed for a lifetime.

This portfolio includes a story about Nina wondering if she is in heaven, a photo of a beautiful two-by-three-foot painting (at the right) and twenty-six gorgeous desert photographs taken near Phoenix, Arizona.

Unlike many picture books, the text is unrelated to the art. This might seem a little weird at first. One thing that helps is to order more portfolios until you get used to it. Until then, feel free to draw your own pictures of Nina and her friends on the pages if you like.

Photographs in this book are available in limited editions. See http://www.MarkDahle.com for more information and for previews of upcoming portfolios.

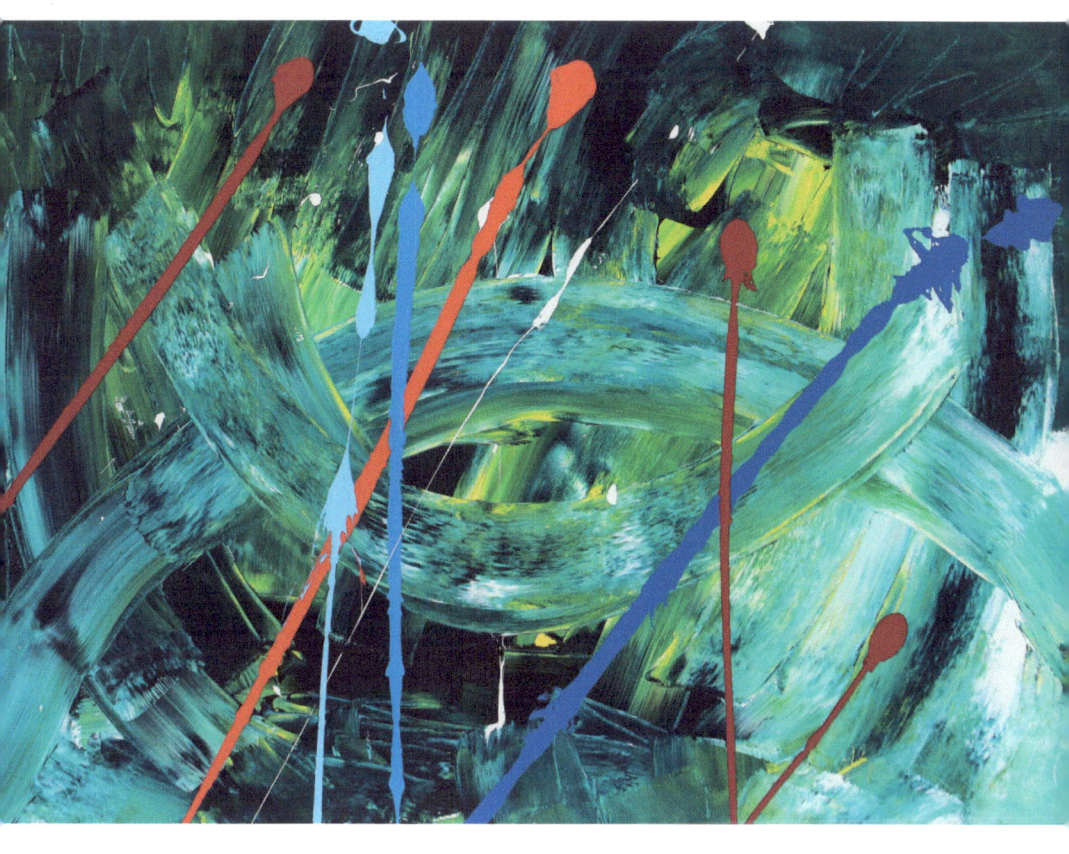

3

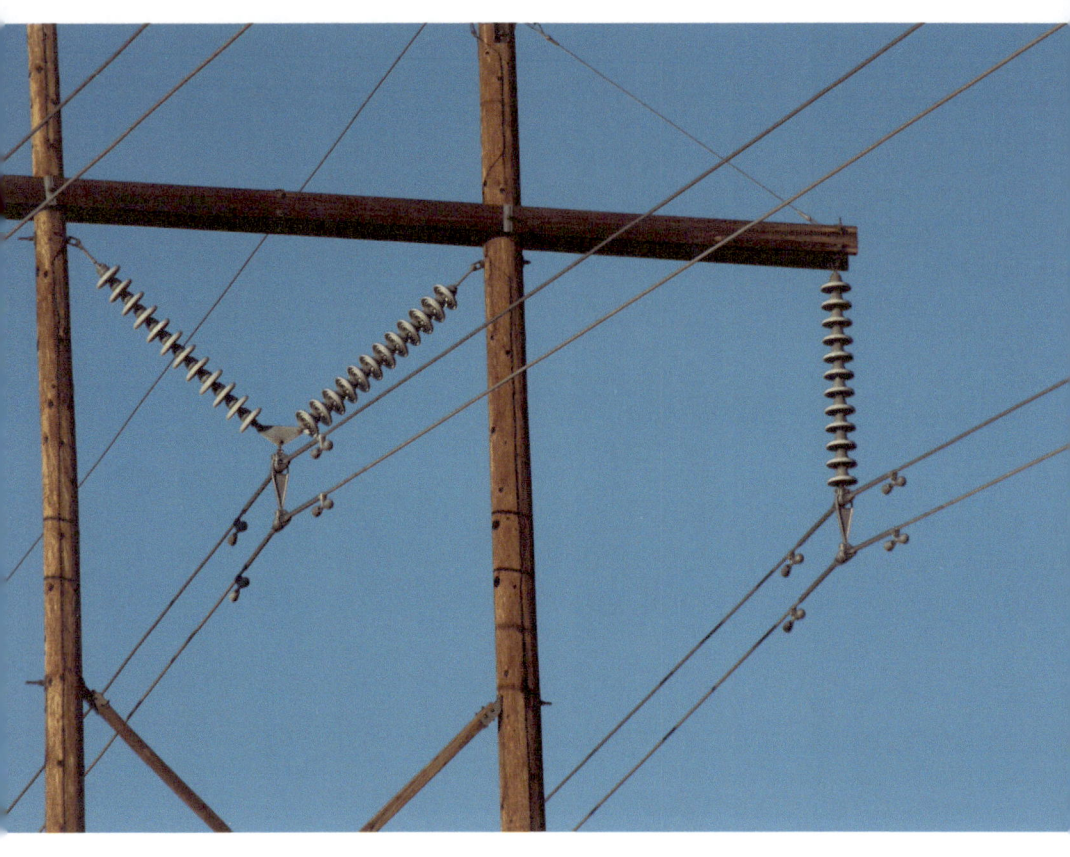

For several centuries after she died,
Nina was quite happy.

But her happiness started to fade
when she began wondering
if – maybe –
she was somewhere other than heaven.

When Nina first had the thought,
she discarded it immediately.

It didn't make sense –
how could she be so happy
and not in heaven?

But as the evidence grew (and grew), she came to
believe that it was at least *possible* that she was
someplace unpleasant. And at this, she became
more and more unhappy, until her spirits finally
matched her gloomy thoughts.

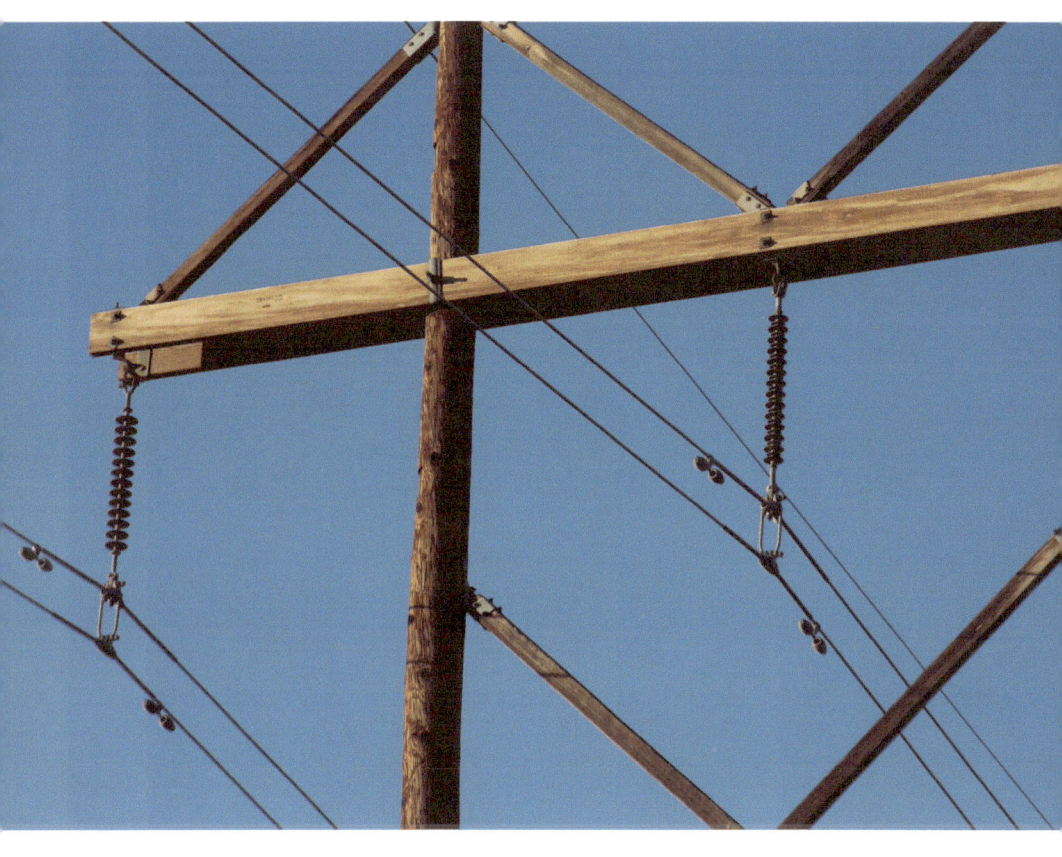

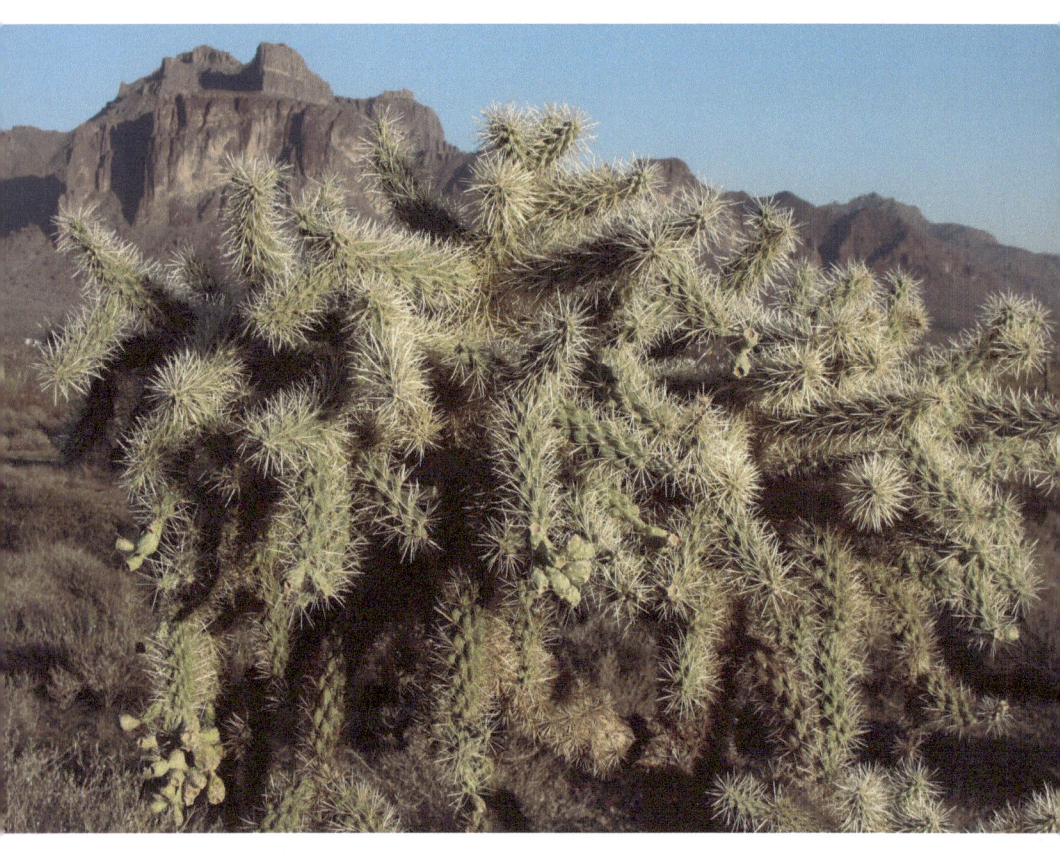

It had started out innocently enough.

For the first few hundred years after she died, Nina had talked with thousands of people who had wild and unusual and entertaining stories. She loved hearing about their adventures – and they convinced her to have so many wonderful and amazing adventures of her own that she hadn't even thought about her old group of friends.

But once she finally *did* think of her old friends, she began to wonder where they might be and why she had not seen any of them yet and how they might be getting along.

Nina had been so unusually happy up to that point that it never occurred to her to look for someone other than the people she was with. She had found her new friends so delightful, so interesting and so curious that she hadn't thought about her past at all. But when she finally *did* start to think about her old friends, she decided to look for Rose.

Rose was the president of the Bible Study group that Nina had been in. If there was anybody in the group who could tell Nina how the rest of the Bible Study members were doing, it was Rose. Rose knew everything about everybody. Nina decided to look her up.

As Nina focused more on finding Rose, something curious happened. Since her attention was diverted from her immediate surroundings, Nina stopped paying as much attention to the people right in front of her. And when she stopped paying close attention to how delightful they were, she began to notice that each of them was a little bit odd. In fact, some of them were *quite a bit* odd.

Everywhere she went, she met people who were – well – shocking in some way.

Even the people who seemed normal at first had something about them that should have disqualified them from getting into heaven. Most had several dozen things like that.

The more Nina looked for Rose, the more she saw the people she was meeting though Rose's eyes. As that happened more and more, Nina realized that the people around her didn't seem very much like Rose at all. In fact, the people she was meeting seemed like the kind of people that Rose would avoid as much as possible.

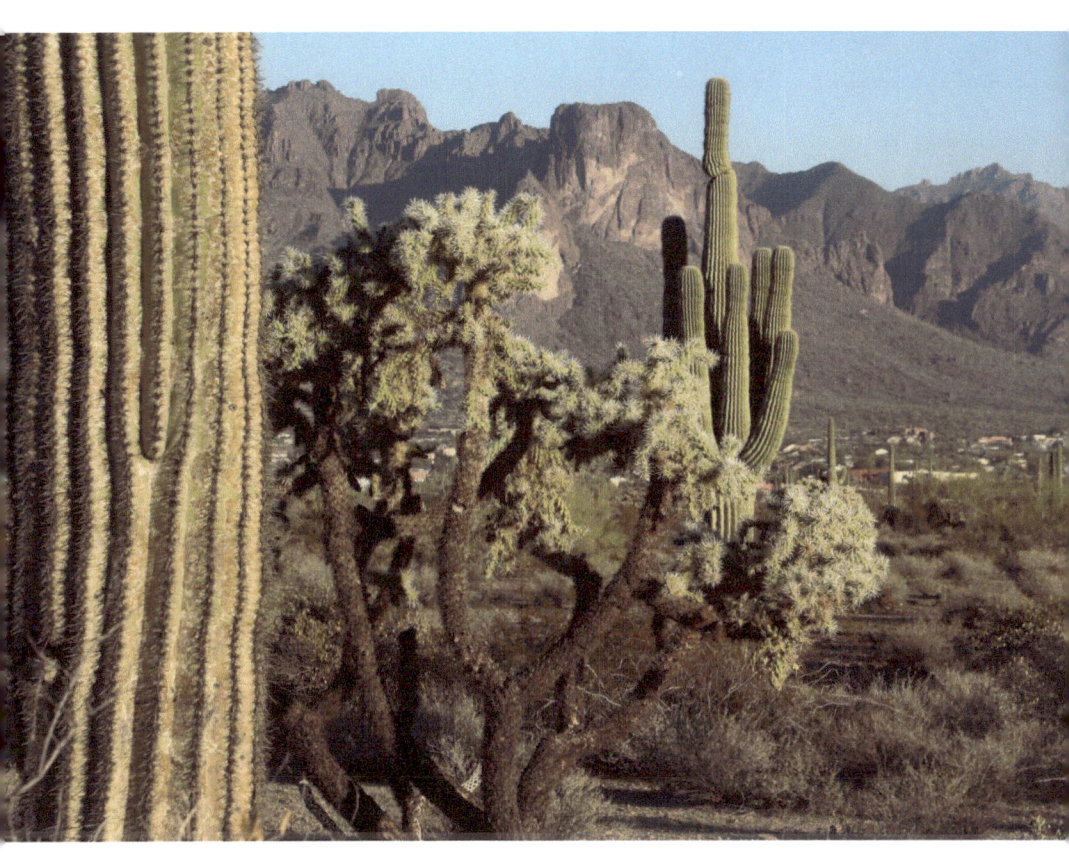

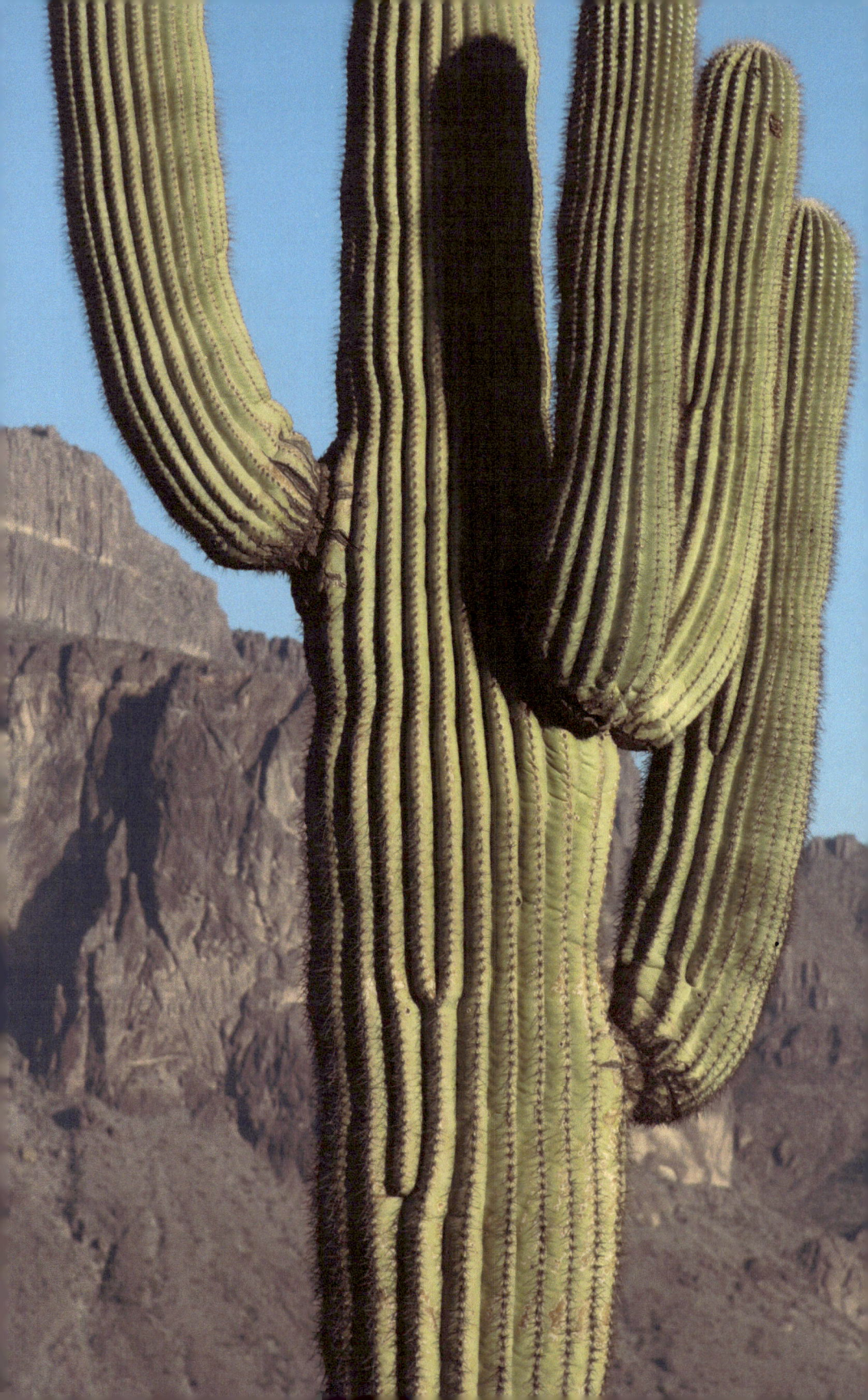

Earlier, Nina had enjoyed meeting
all these unusual people.

But now it occurred to her that almost everyone
in the place where she was – which she had
previously thought was heaven – was someone
that Rose wouldn't want to know.

For the next few days,
Nina kept up her search for Rose,
asking people, one at a time,
if they had seen her.

No one had.

After a week or a month
or some amount of time,
(it's hard to tell in eternity)
it finally occurred to Nina
that this way of looking for Rose
was way too slow.

Nina knew she had as much time as she wanted,
but what she wanted was something faster.

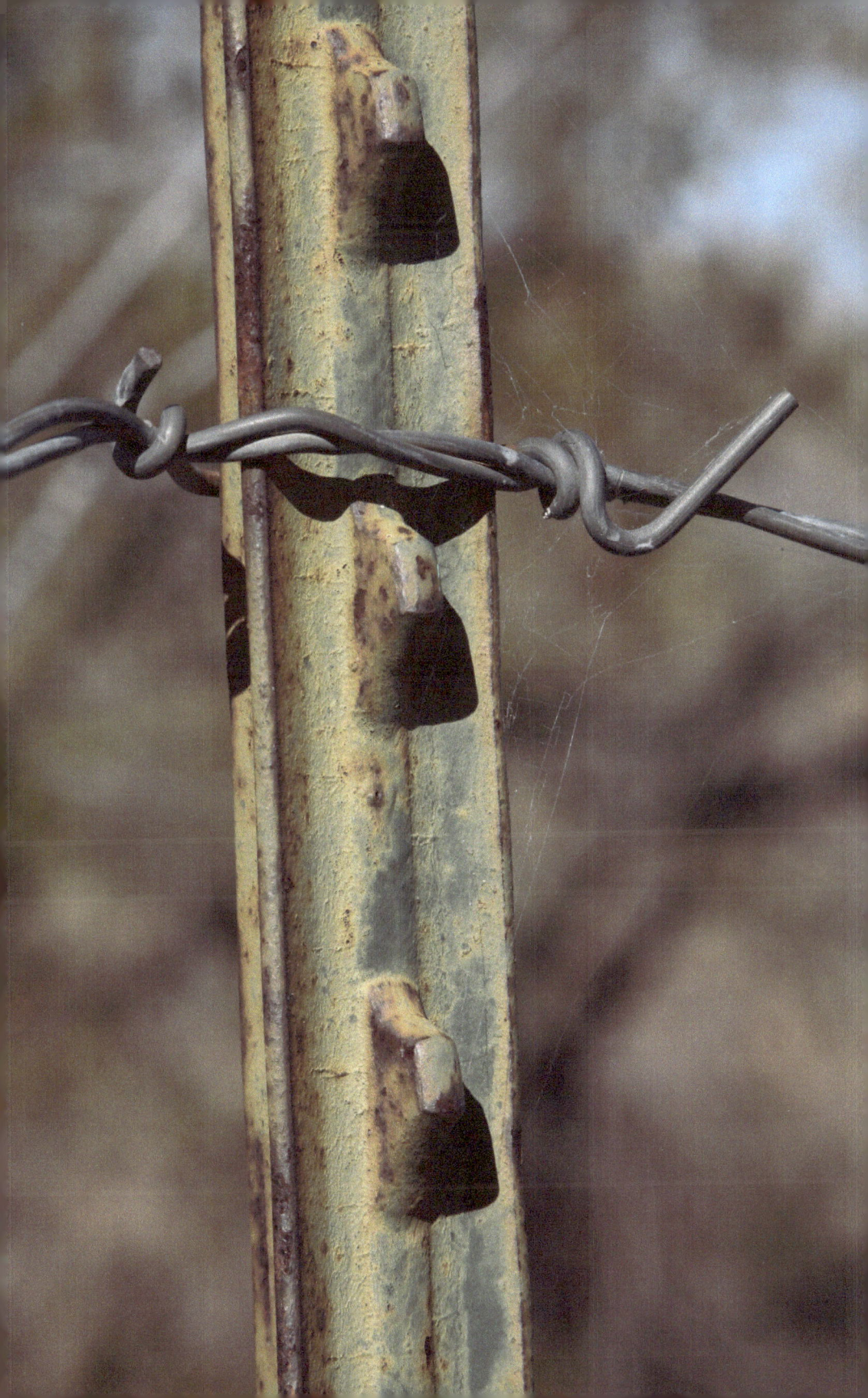

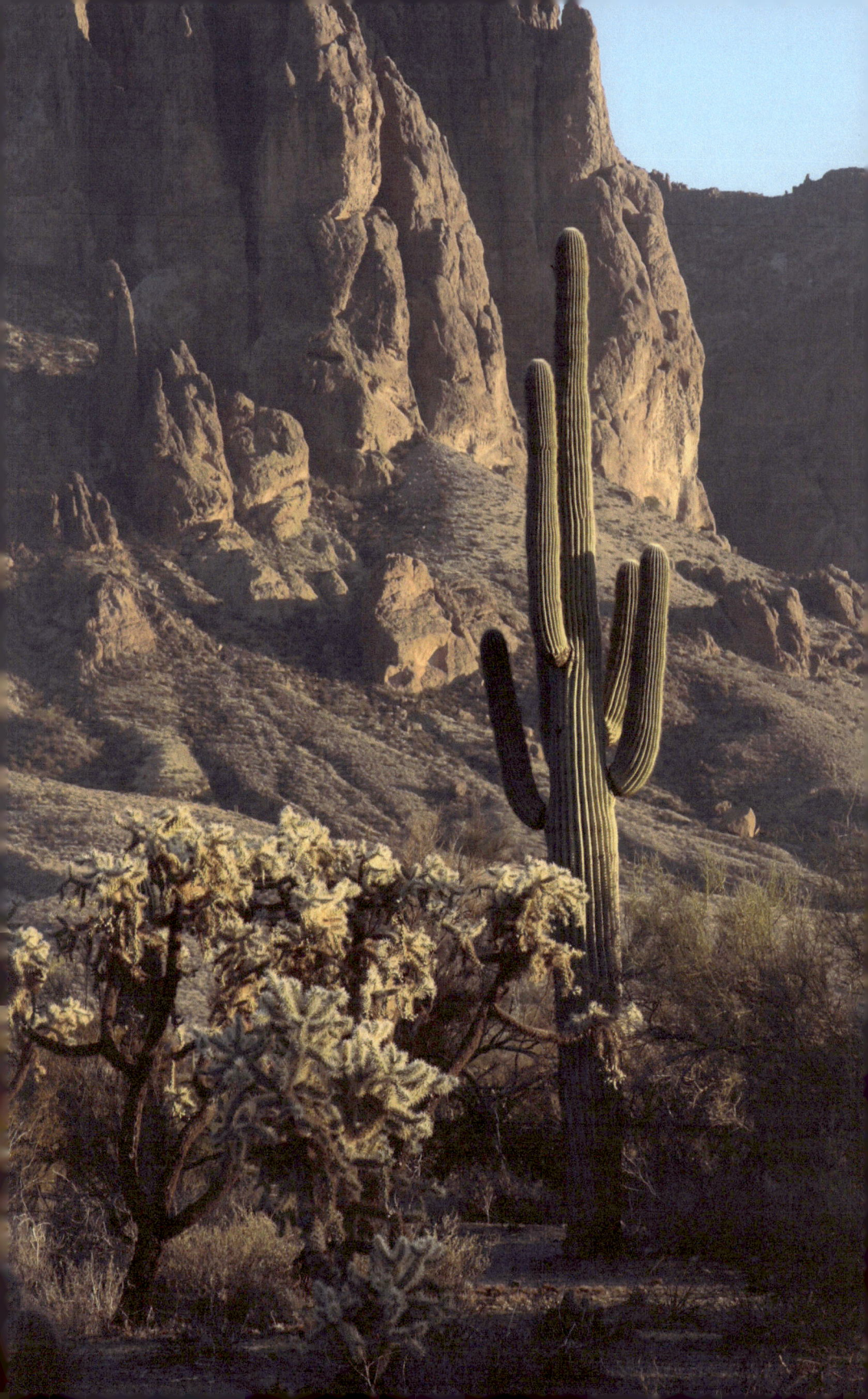

Before she had died, Nina had heard
that St. Peter was at the entrance to heaven,
checking everybody in
(as if he had nothing better to do).

Nina decided to consult St. Peter
and ask if he knew where Rose was.

So one morning, early, she headed for the
entrance.

When she arrived,
Nina went straight to the person in charge
and asked if he were Peter.

He laughed out loud.

"Pete?" he said, still laughing.
"Peter is *not* a numbers guy.
He couldn't keep up with the data *centuries* ago.
He's off fishing."

Then his appearance became more somber.
"Look. You wanted to know about Rose.
I have some news that you weren't expecting:
She's not here."

Nina was dumbstruck,
She was so surprised she just repeated
what he'd said, except she asked it as a question.

"Rose isn't here?"

"No," Matthew said.
"She's next door. Across the chasm."

"Across the chasm?" Nina repeated.

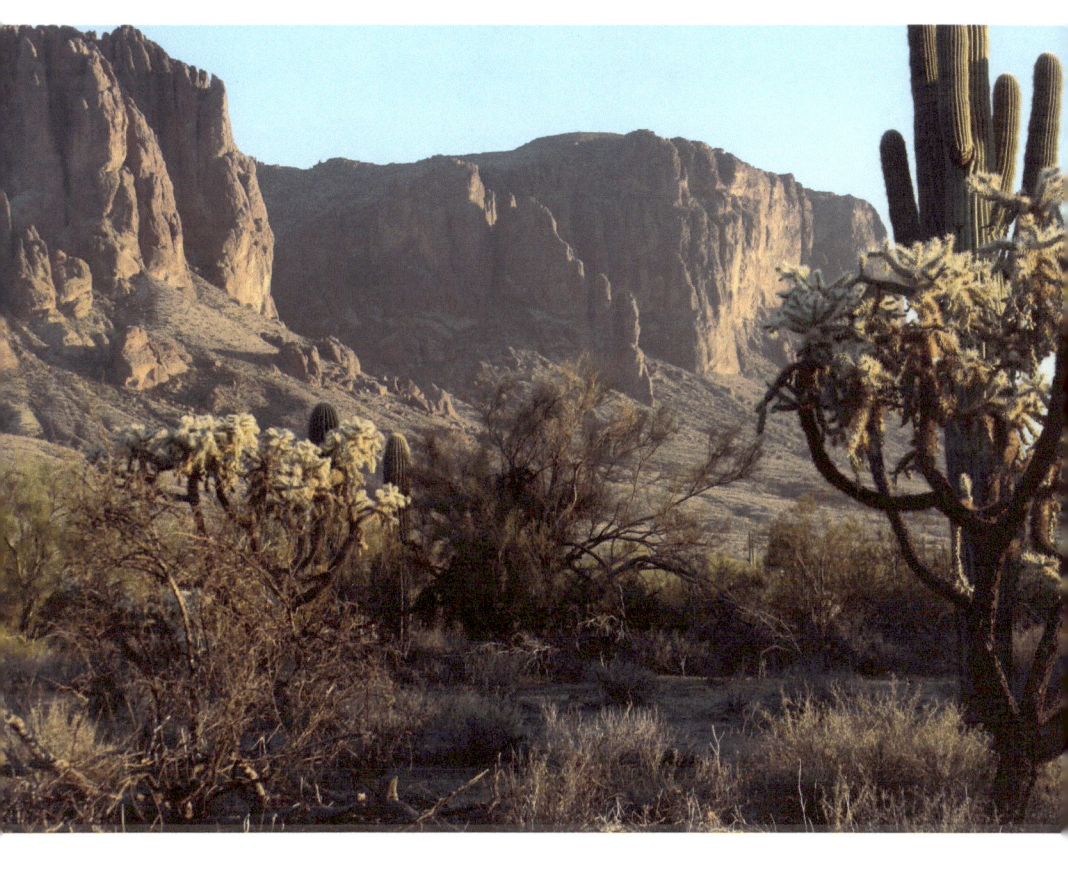

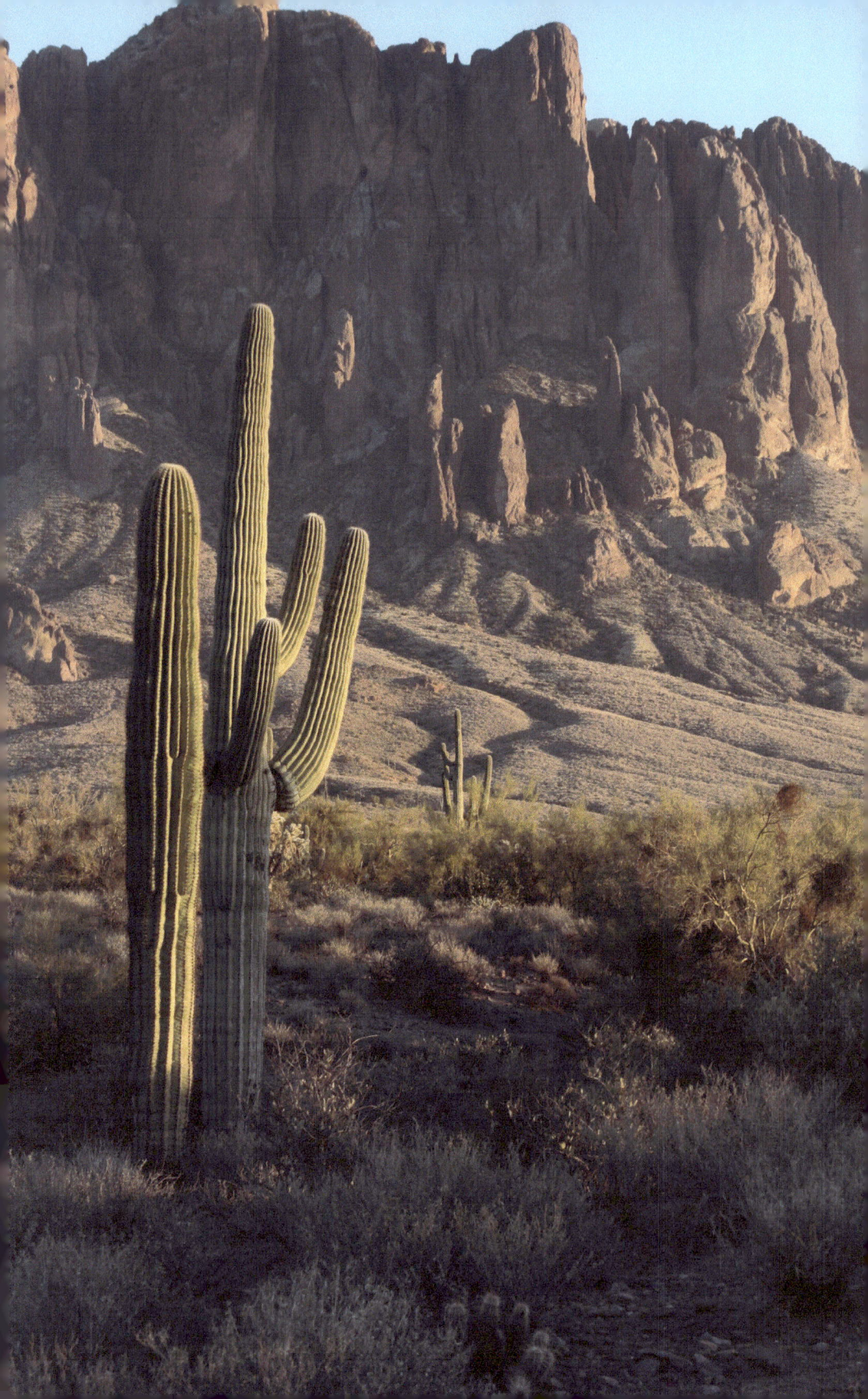

Nina couldn't think of anything else to say.
She just stumbled backwards
and headed for home.

When she arrived at her house –
which up until now had always seemed so perfect
for her – she just sat in a daze.

How it could happen
that Rose was not in heaven?

And if Rose was across the chasm,
where could *Nina* be?

That thought was the first in the chain
that led to the idea that maybe,
possibly,
somehow
Nina was the one who wasn't in heaven.

The more Nina thought about this problem, the more she realized that all the wild and wonderful people she had been meeting might be the sort of people that you'd find, well, *not* in heaven. Someplace else.

But how could Nina have been so happy meeting all these different and unusual people if she weren't in heaven? Nina couldn't figure it out. She turned it over and over in her mind for days.

She kept coming back to this:
Rose was the *President* of the Bible Study.
How could she not be in the same place that Nina was? If anyone got to go to heaven,
it ought to be the President of the Bible Study.

Finally Nina got up the nerve
to go back and ask Matthew another question.

Sheri was the Vice President of the Bible Study. If anybody would know about the other members of the group and how they were doing – someone other than Rose – it was Sheri. Sheri knew nearly as much about everybody as Rose. Nina decided to find her.

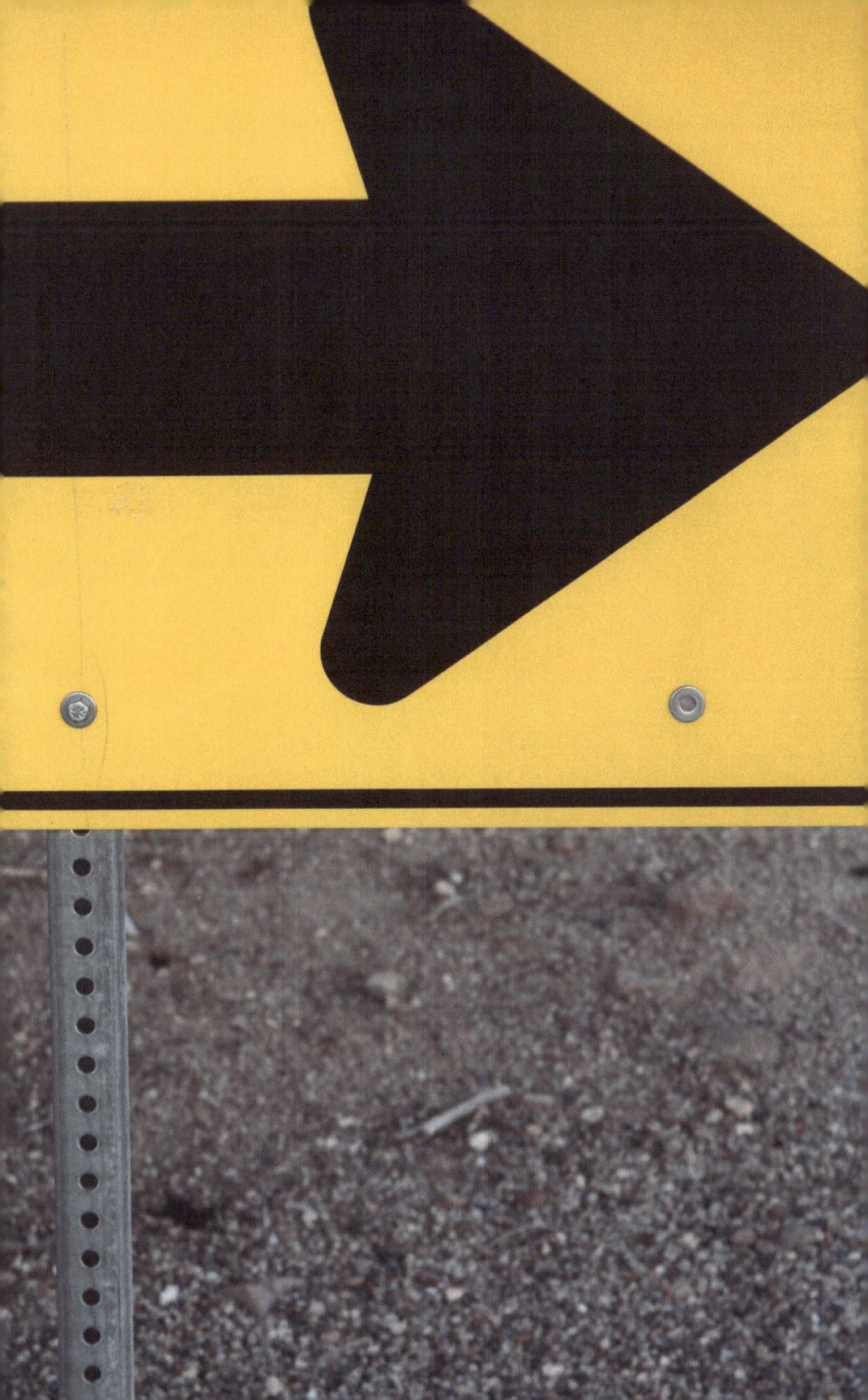

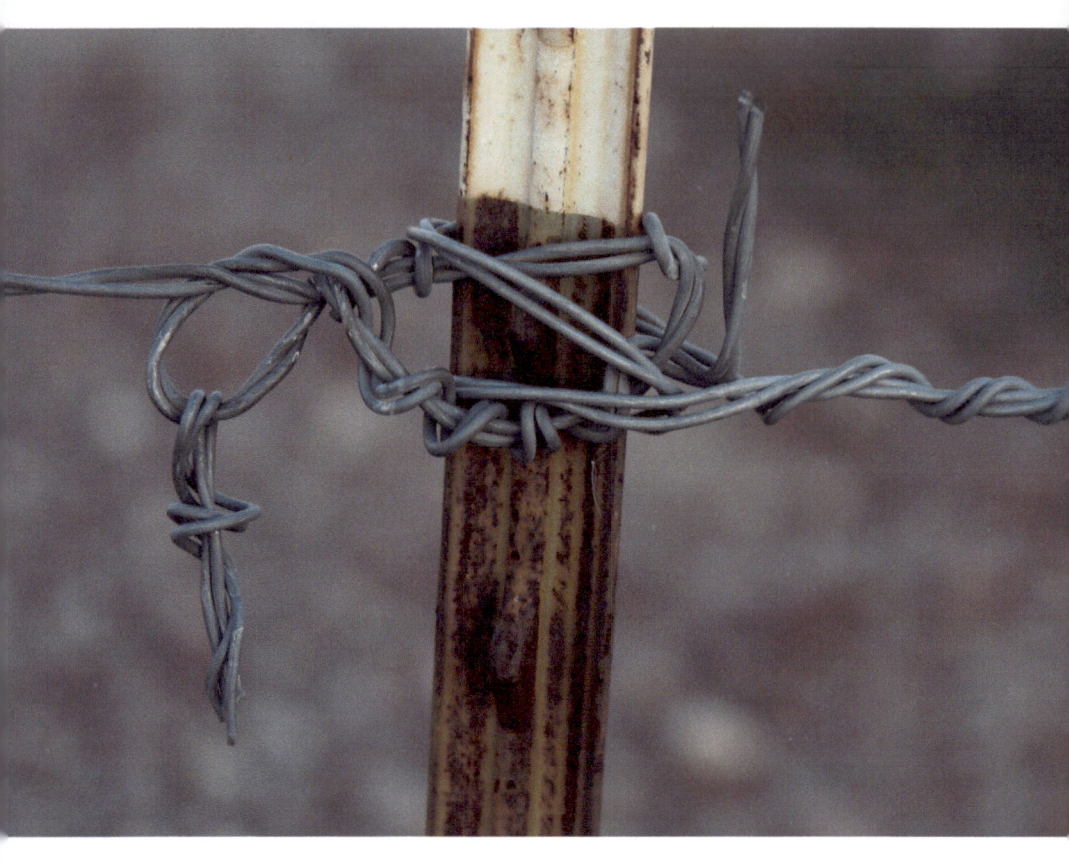

It took Nina some time to make the trek back to the main entrance. She started out several times but kept turning around when she was half way, not wanting to be shocked like before.

But she finally decided she *had* to know and set off, reluctantly.

When she arrived,
Matthew looked up from his books and smiled.
"Oh, hi Nina.
I bet you're wondering about Sheri."

Nina's eyes widened,
and she nodded.

"I'm sorry Nina.
I have bad news there, too.
Sheri's not here either.
She's with Rose."

Matthew looked into her eyes with compassion.

"Look," he said. "I know you have all eternity
to work on this, but I'll save you some time.
Everybody else from the Bible Study is across the
chasm, too. You're the only one here."

He looked at her kindly a second longer, and then
went back to his books.

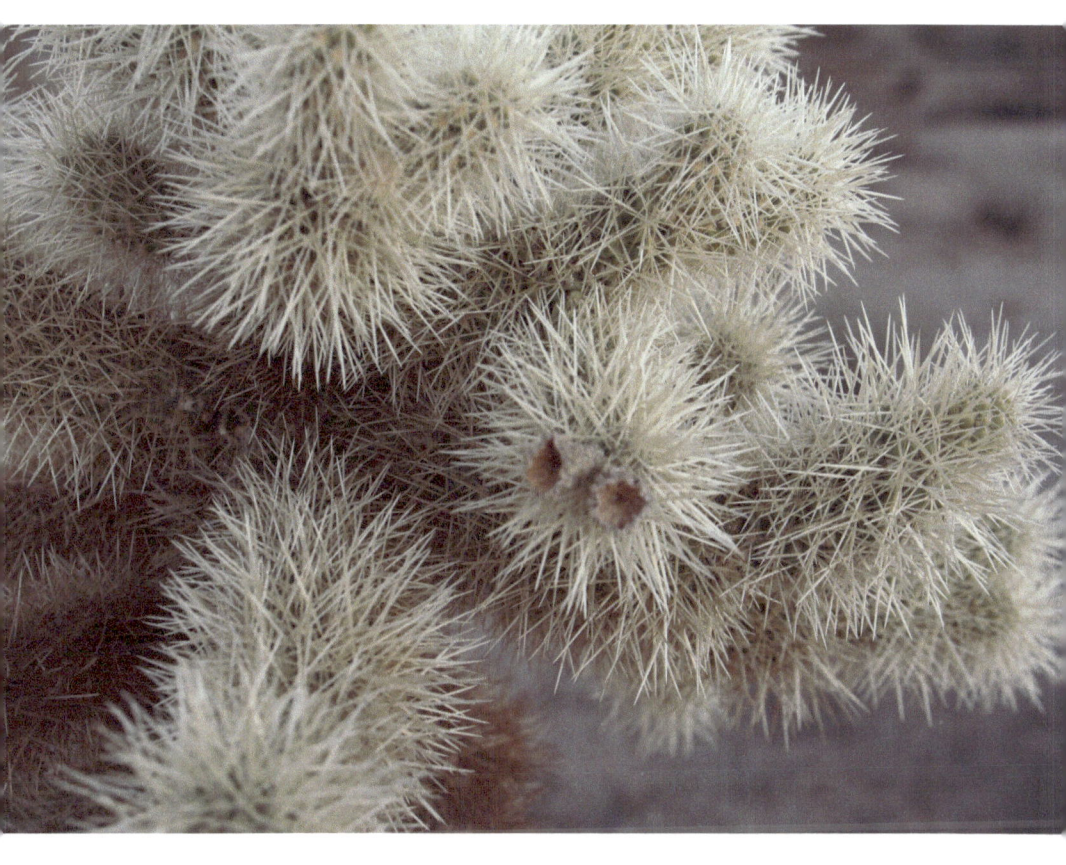

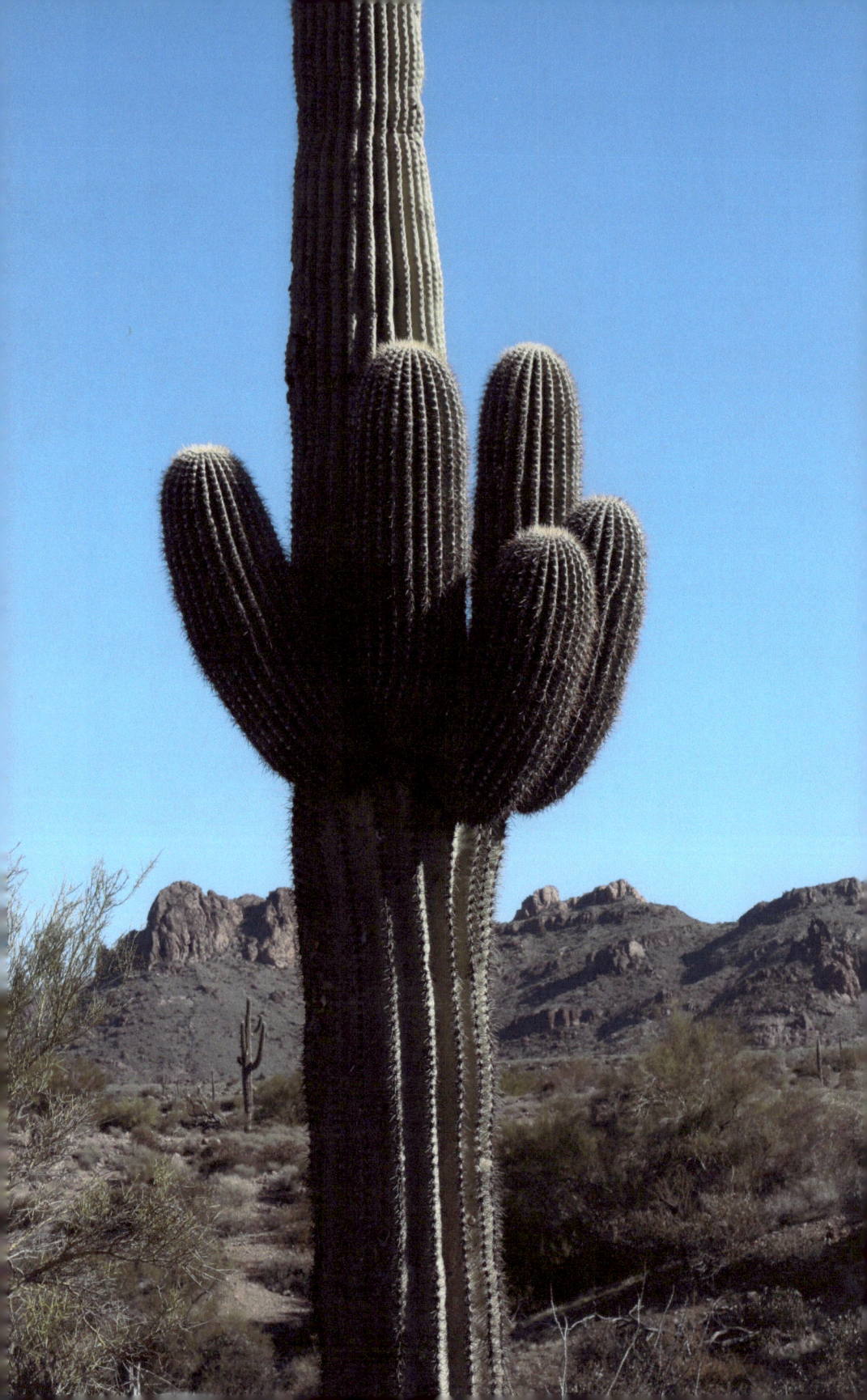

Nina backed up slowly,
unsteadily.
She didn't even say thank you.

Before, Nina could barely fathom that Rose hadn't made it into heaven. When Matthew told her that Rose *and* Sheri hadn't made it, it had been another staggering blow. But *nobody* else from the group had made it?

Nina slowly walked home,
and for the first time
what looked like it wanted to be a tear
tried to form in her eyes.
If Rose wasn't here
and Sheri wasn't here
and everybody else from the group wasn't here,
where was Nina?

Nina had only seen the chasm once. It was frighteningly vast.

Millennia ago it had looked impossible to cross. But one day a bridge had appeared.

It happened so suddenly, it caught people on both sides by surprise. First there wasn't a bridge, then one day there was.

The bridge looked safe,
strong, well-built, and secure,
even though it was completely transparent.
So on the day it first appeared,
lots of curious people tested it out.
But since then it had been mostly abandoned.

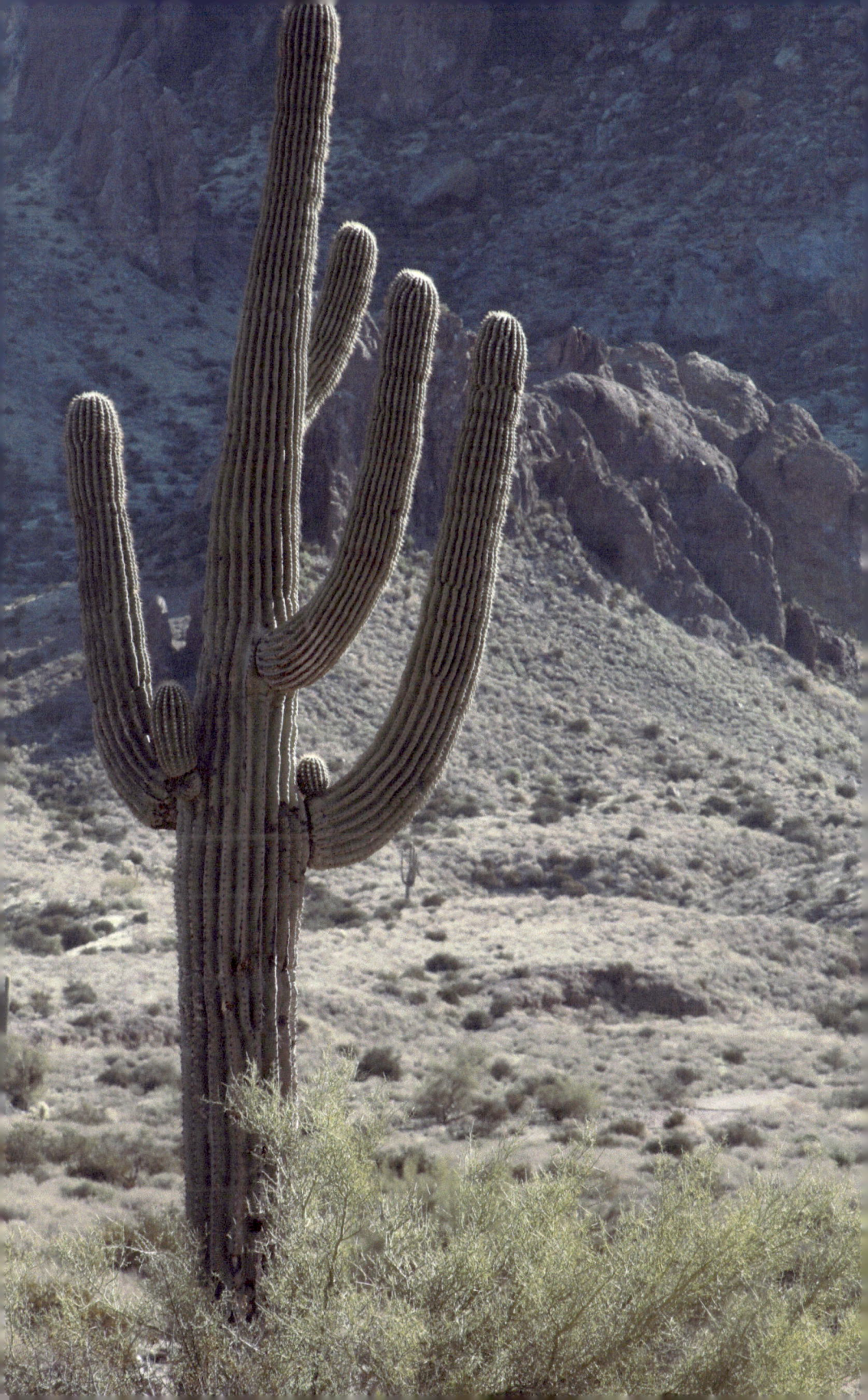

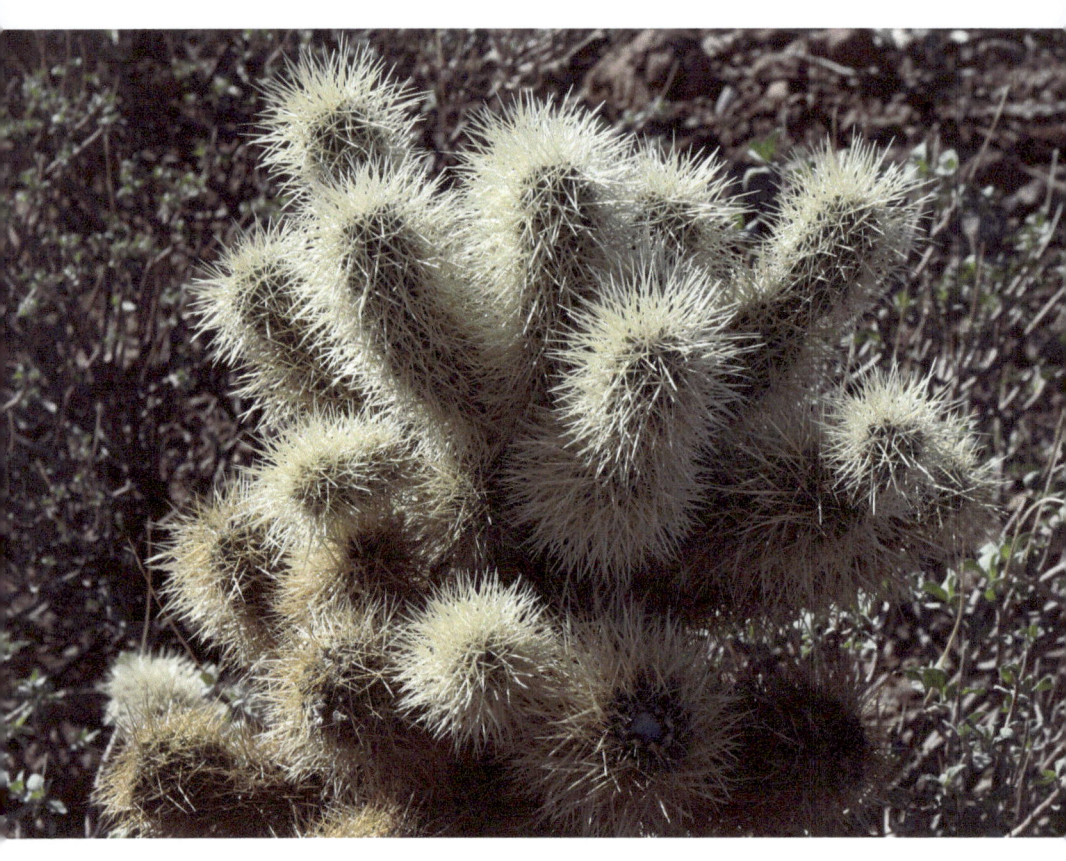

Nina went to the bridge and stepped onto it gingerly. It felt solid. But since it was made of glass (or something like it), with every step you had a clear view of the immense distance down to the bottom of the chasm and a clear view of the immense distance across to the other side. Nina took a few terrified steps. The bridge seemed sturdy. With each step she took, Nina gained confidence.

It took a long time to cross. But when she finally reached the other side, Nina found the path was wide and easy to travel, although the air wasn't very good. The air had a gritty, acidic feel, and there were puffs of smoke in the distance almost everywhere she looked. The temperature grew warmer as she walked, and soon was quite unpleasant. But Nina didn't have to go far – although in eternity, with all the time in the world to do things, it's hard to tell how much time things really take and how far apart they really are.

At any rate, after what seemed like a short amount of time compared with the time she had, Nina found her friends sitting around a table having coffee.

"Nina!" Rose shouted. "We've been wondering what happened to you. Come join us!"
And there were Rose and Sheri
and all the rest waving eagerly
for her to come and sit with them.

"We've been having the best Bible Study ever," said Sheri. "It's just heavenly! You've no idea how much better it can be when you've got centuries to study and talk."

Sheri looked Nina over. "You've missed so much!" she said. "But I'm sure you'll catch up after just a few years. We've got a chair just for you right here."

At that point, something curious happened. When Nina had started looking at the people on the other side of the bridge while thinking about Rose, she had seen them as Rose might see them. Now, when looking at Rose and Sheri and the rest, Nina saw her old friends as they probably appeared to Matthew and some of the people on the other side of the chasm. And somehow the Bible Study group didn't look quite so appealing as she had remembered.

Nina couldn't explain her reaction. It didn't make sense exactly. Mostly she just felt it in her stomach. But they looked a little thin, a little wispy, a little like they were starting to disappear. And most of them didn't look quite as nice as she remembered, even though they were all trying very hard to smile.

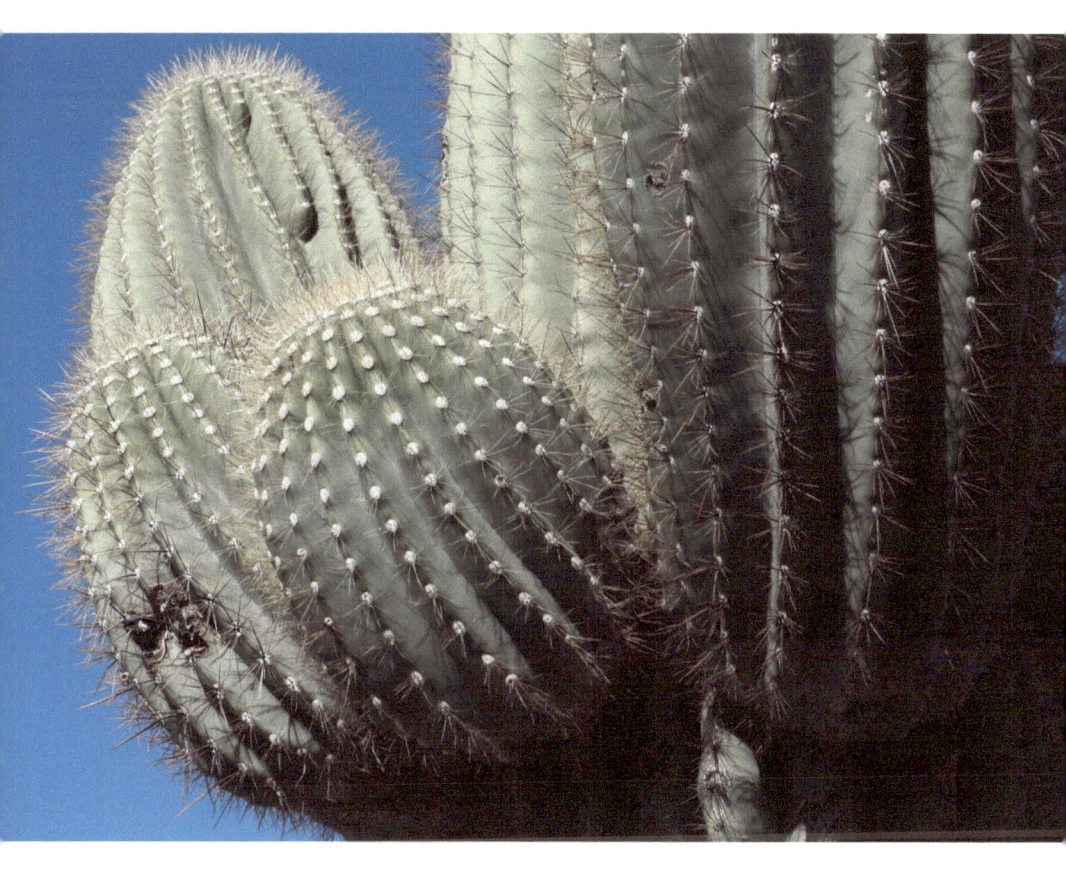

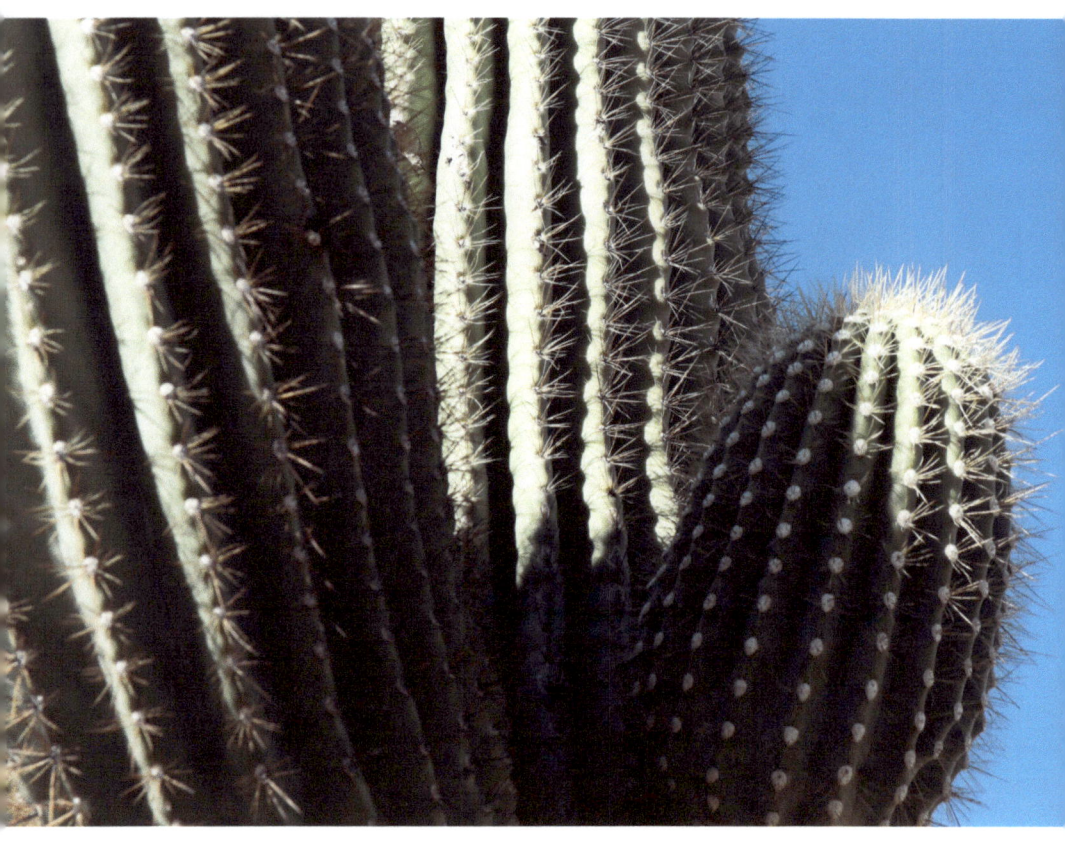

Ever since she had arrived on this side of
the bridge, Nina had felt a growing sense of
uneasiness. Maybe it was just the bad air.

But now that she had found her old friends,
Nina was even more uncomfortable.

She backed up, just a little.
First one step, then another,
back towards the bridge.

Each step she took, her old friends
looked a little more appalling –
a little more thin and a little less friendly,
a little less comfortable.

They were still calling to her,
but spending time with them
no longer seemed as important
as she had thought.
"I think maybe you should come with me," she said.
"I think you should have some adventures
on the other side of the bridge."

She was still backing up as she said it.

"Across the bridge?" Rose snorted. "We'd *never* go there. That bridge is *way* too frightning."

Nina was still backing up, and she suddenly realized she had a choice.

She could study the Bible for all eternity with her old friends on this side of the bridge.

Or she could spend eternity having adventures with the strange people she had grown to love on the other side.

It didn't take more than a second to decide. "If you change your minds you know where I am," she shouted.

Then she turned towards the bridge and ran full tilt, afraid it might disappear before she could get back across.

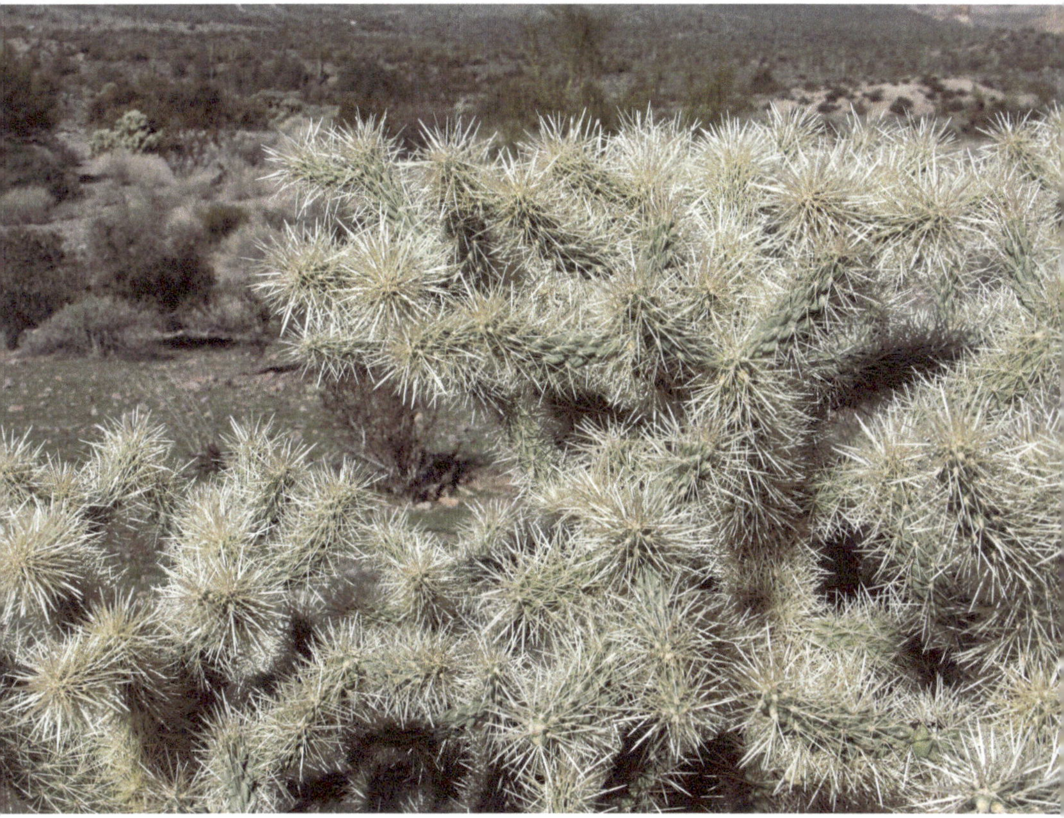
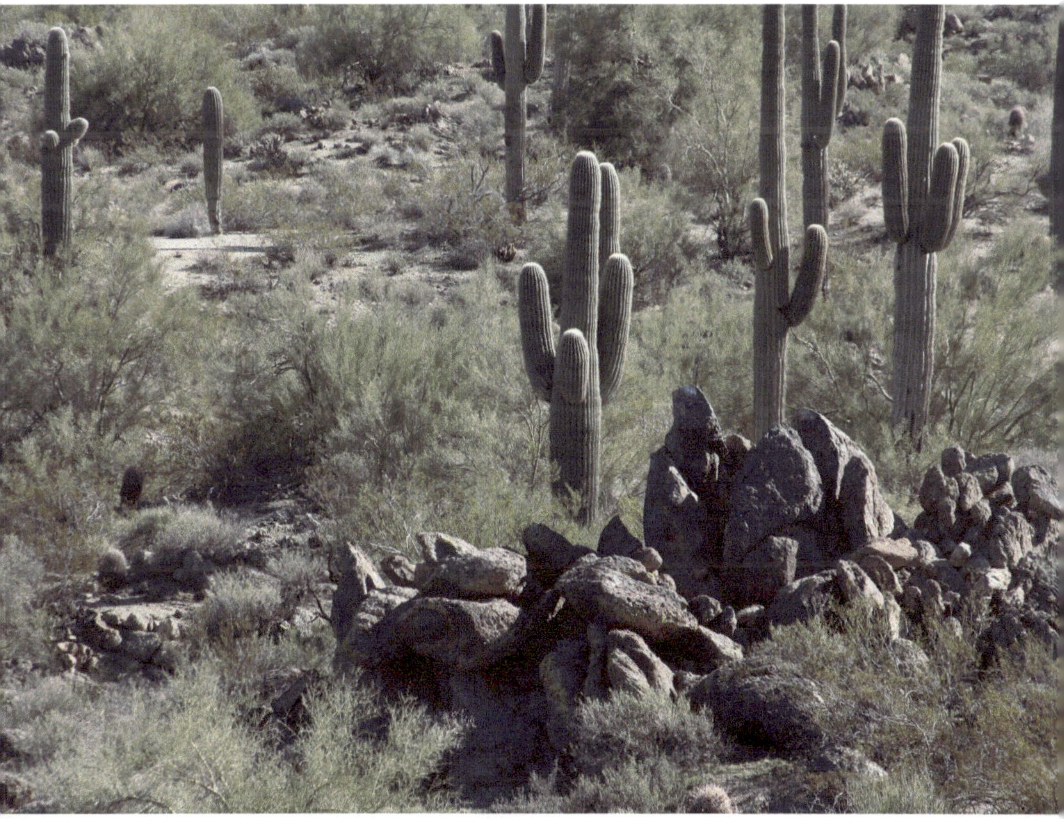

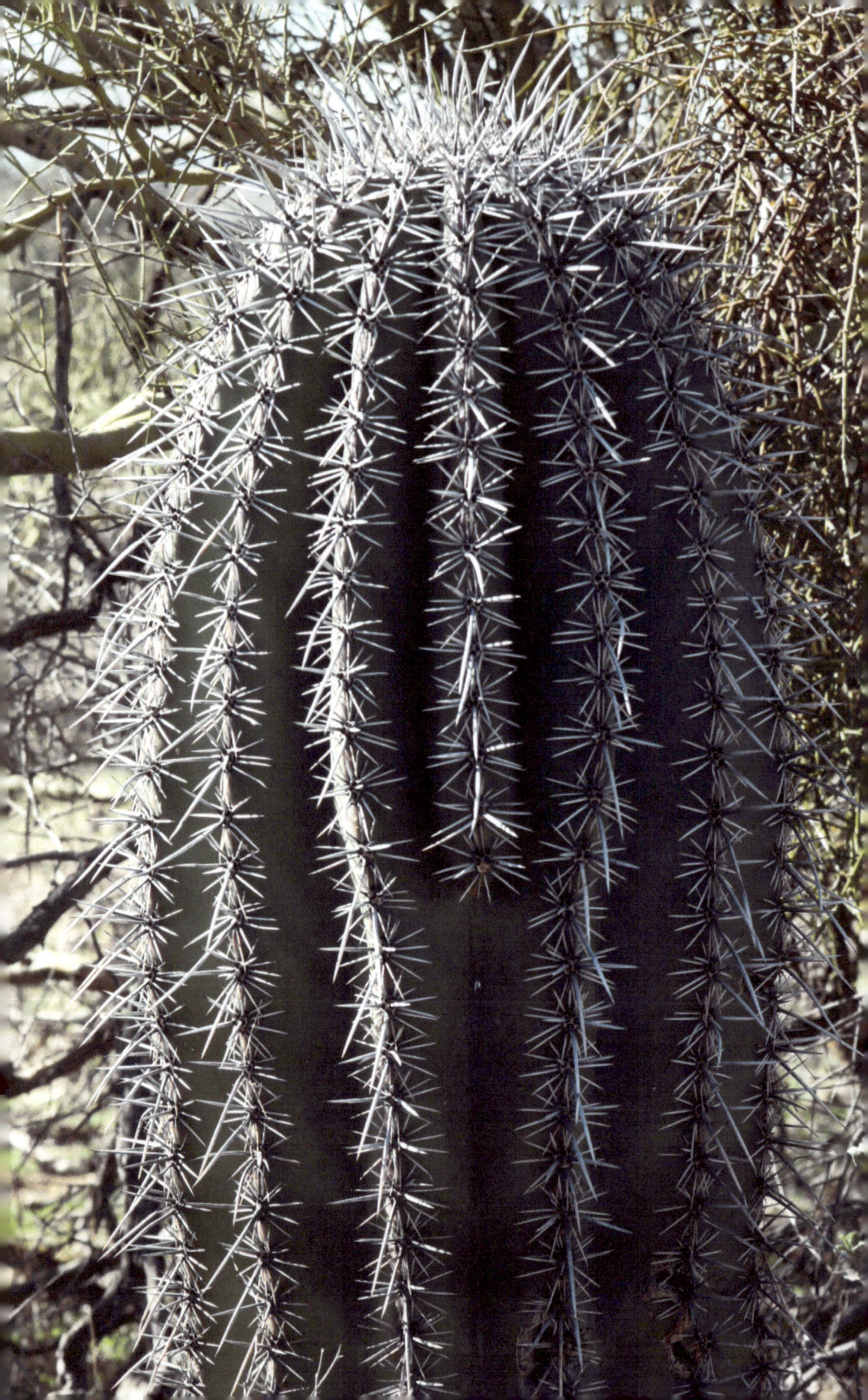

"Nina," her old friends called as she fled.
"Come back. You can stay with us.
A little study will do you good.
You're part of this group.
We've got your space right here.
Come sit with us."

But she was fleeing for her life and was not really at peace until her feet were finally back on the side where she had started.

Before she had died, Nina had always looked up to Rose and Sheri. They had seemed so amazing with all they knew about the Bible. But seeing them after having had centuries of adventures, they almost appeared frightening. It's true that they had all eternity to learn more (and more and more) about the Bible. But on her side of the bridge Nina felt like she was probably living it, without really studying it all that much. And having tasted both, she liked living it much better.

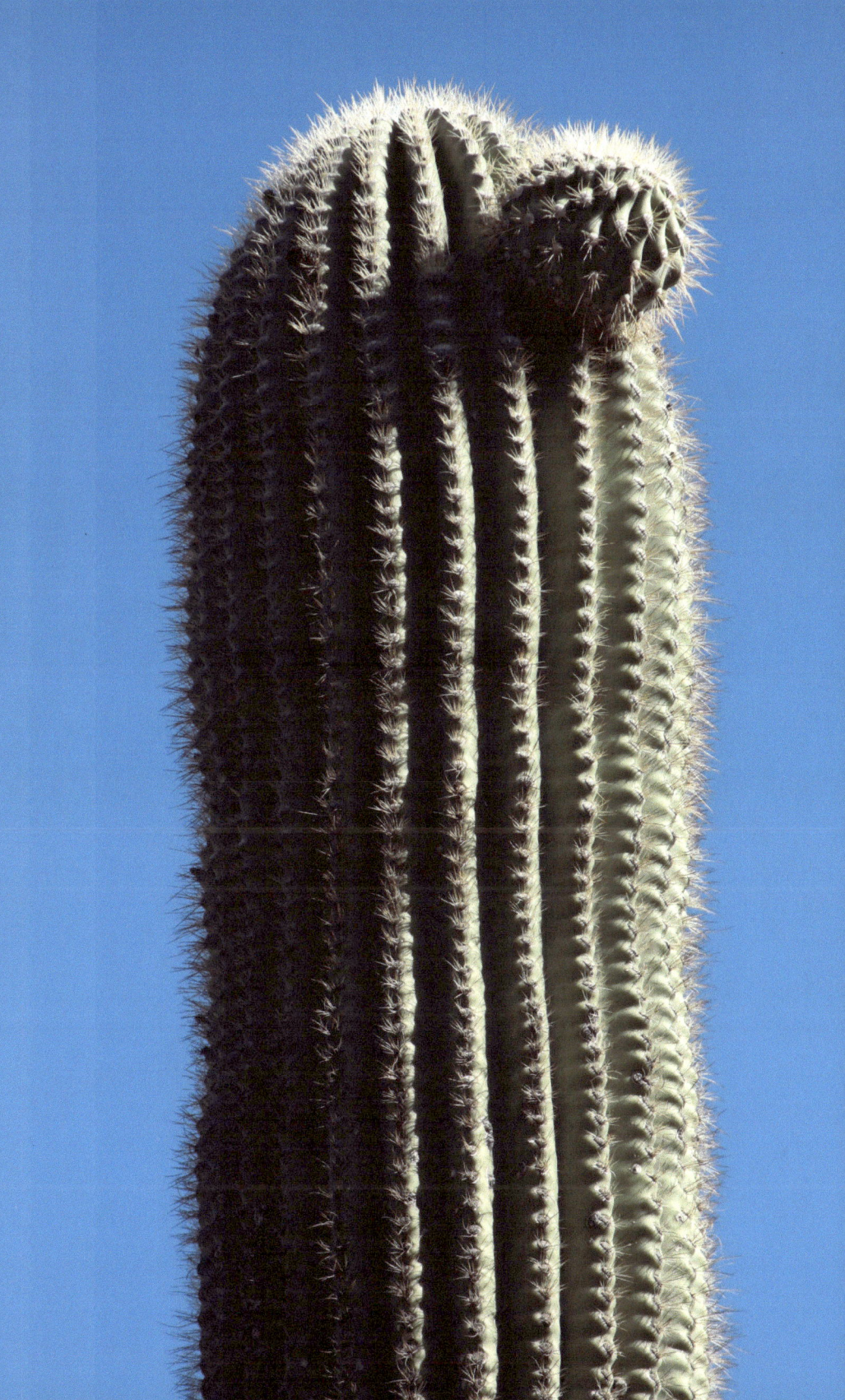

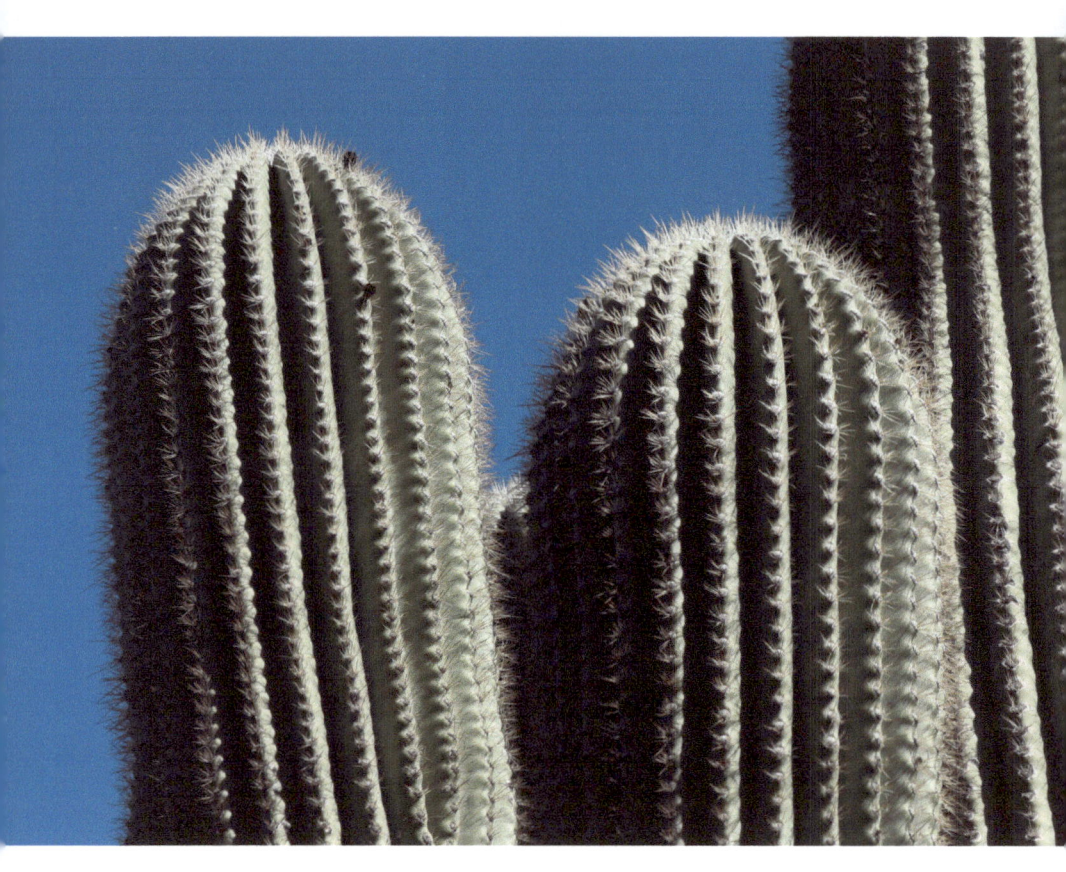

Some time later, Nina took one more trip to see Matthew.

"Did you know," she asked, "that the bridge over the chasm makes it easy for people to get from here to there?"

Matthew looked up from his books.

"Well," he said, "if you mean 'easy'
as in, 'a person can cross
without breaking a sweat,'
yes, it's remarkably easy.
Physically.
But almost nobody wants to make the trip.
We have very few people
who make the switch,
going either direction.
It's not really that easy, all things considered.
Once people make their choice,
they usually stick with it.

"So yes, there's a bridge.
But aside from the day it was first installed,
it gets very little use."

Nina hesitated, but she felt she *had* to ask.

"It's really not that unpleasant over there," she said. "At least it's not as bad as I had heard."

"You were on the outskirts," Matthew replied. "And there's a lot more of eternity to come. The new day will dawn soon enough."

Nina didn't know what that meant, but she decided she didn't have to know everything. She was certain she would experience it when the time was right.

When she got back to her home, it once more seemed perfect for her. And Nina lost no time starting several new adventures with several new friends.

~

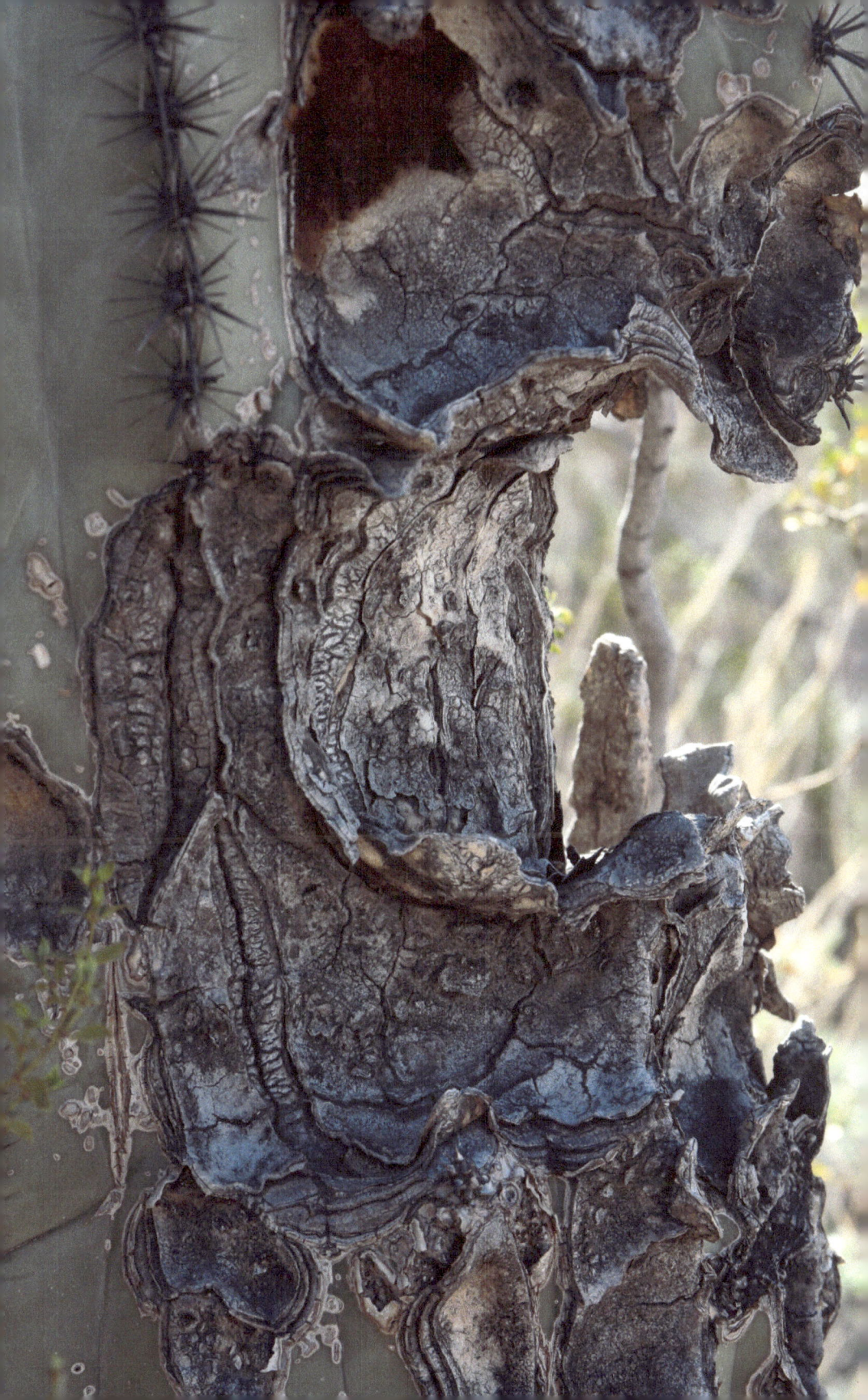

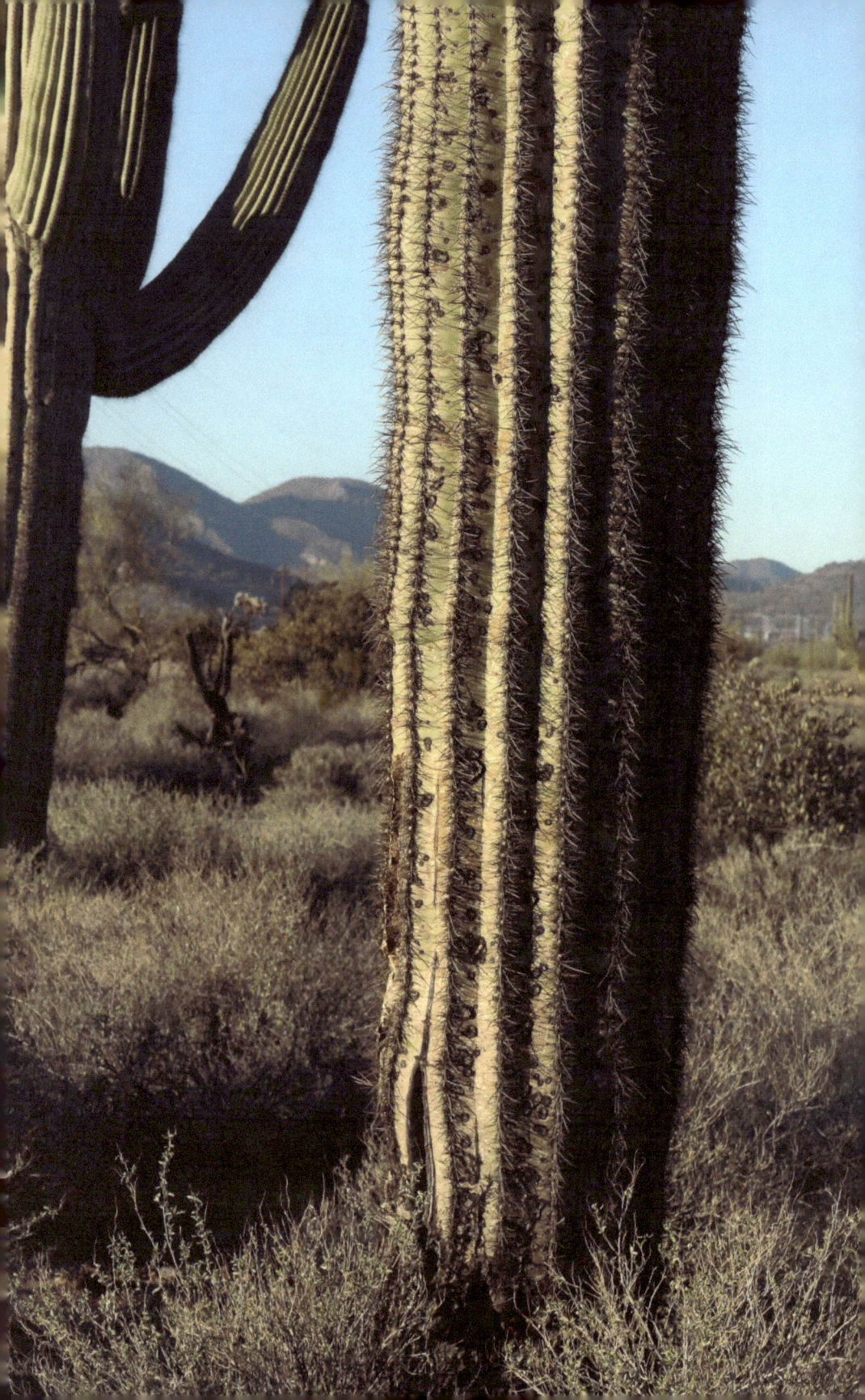

Reflection Questions

Have you ever doubted a good thing?

Did you enjoy it as much when you were doubting?

How much does your attitude about something determine what you feel about it?

Are you more inclined
        a) to study about good things or
        b) to experience them for yourself?

On which side of the chasm do you think you'd be the most comfortable, at least initially?

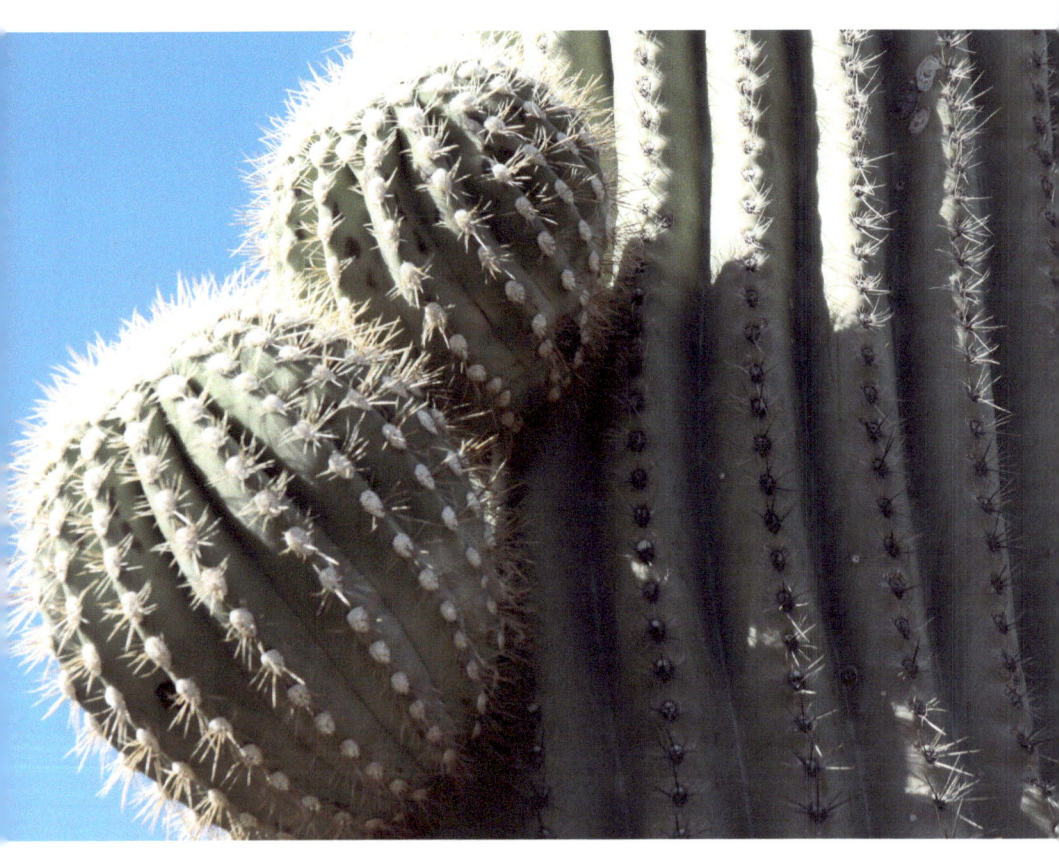

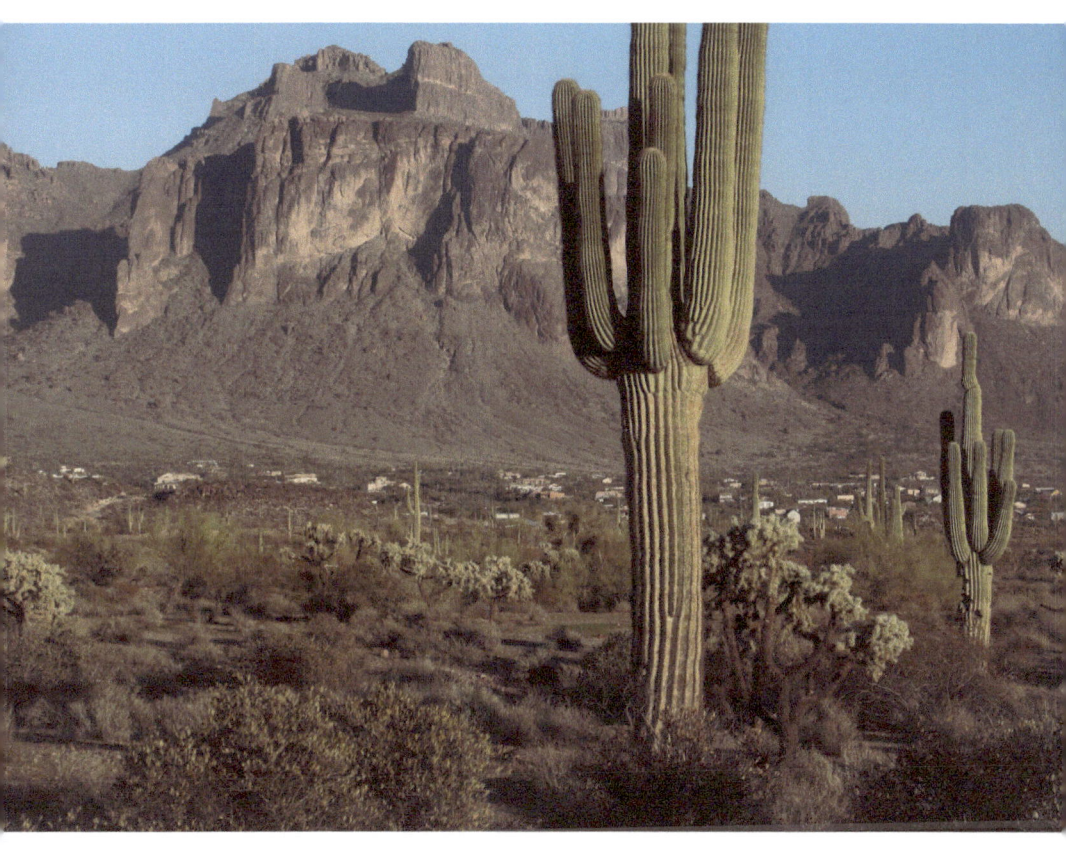

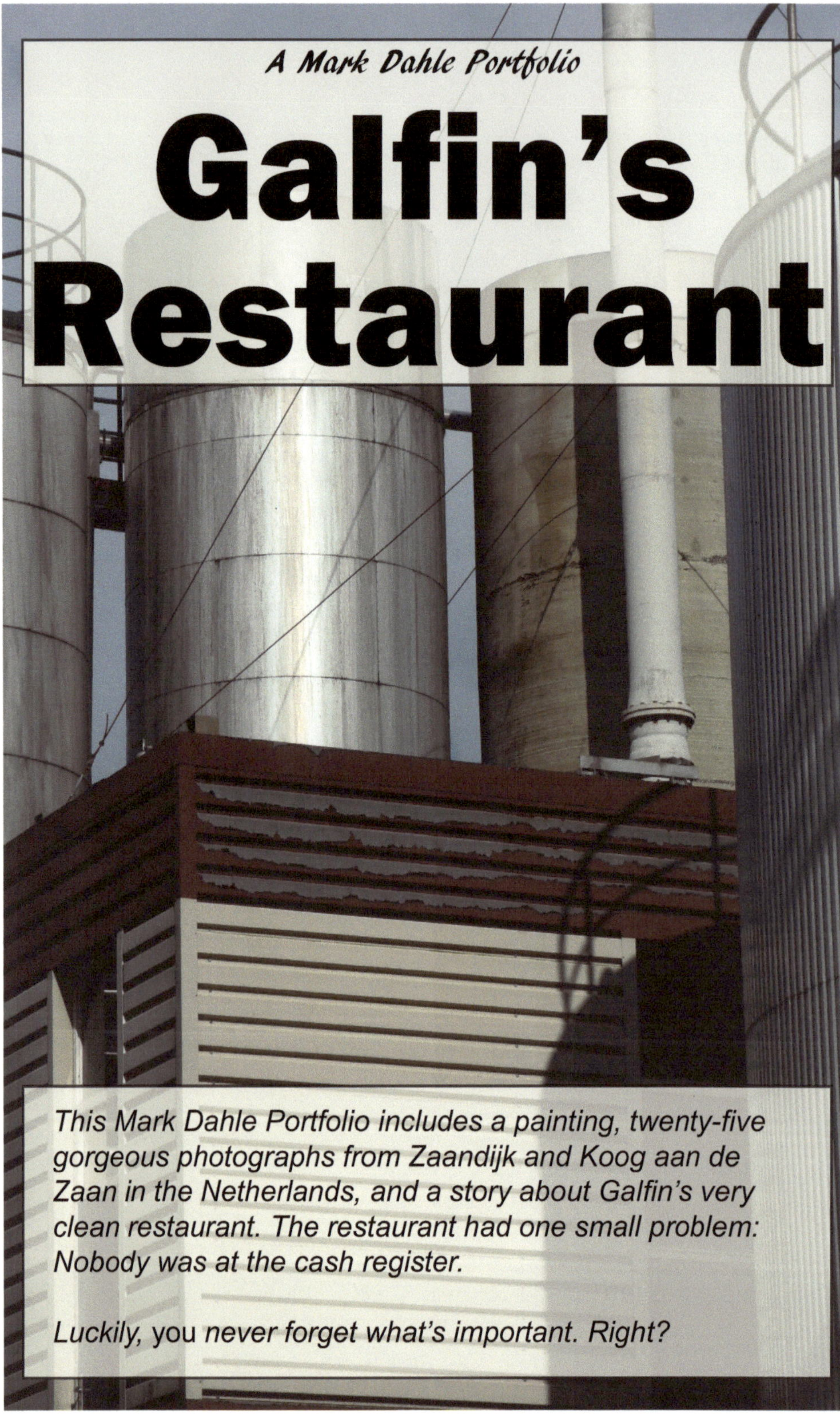

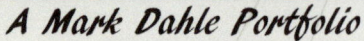

Galfin's Restaurant

This Mark Dahle Portfolio includes a painting, twenty-five gorgeous photographs from Zaandijk and Koog aan de Zaan in the Netherlands, and a story about Galfin's very clean restaurant. The restaurant had one small problem: Nobody was at the cash register.

Luckily, you never forget what's important. Right?

This Mark Dahle Portfolio includes a beautiful painting, twenty-five outstanding photographs from Manhattan, and the story of a busload of hungry passengers on a trip to the best restaurant in the world.

A couple hours into the journey, Jamil stood up and addressed the other passengers.

"Let's not wait," he said. "Let's stop on the way for a little bite – something just to tide us over."

CITY-GATES
QUEENS, N.Y.
718 939·9700

A Mark Dahle Portfolio

Mama Yah's Kitchen

Teri's Renovation

This Mark Dahle Portfolio includes a painting, twenty-five beautiful industrial photos of New York, and a story about the renovation of Teri's house (which was a nightmare).

The contractor is an honest guy, so I'm certain he told Teri all the details, or at least some of them, at least in general. But maybe she wasn't listening.

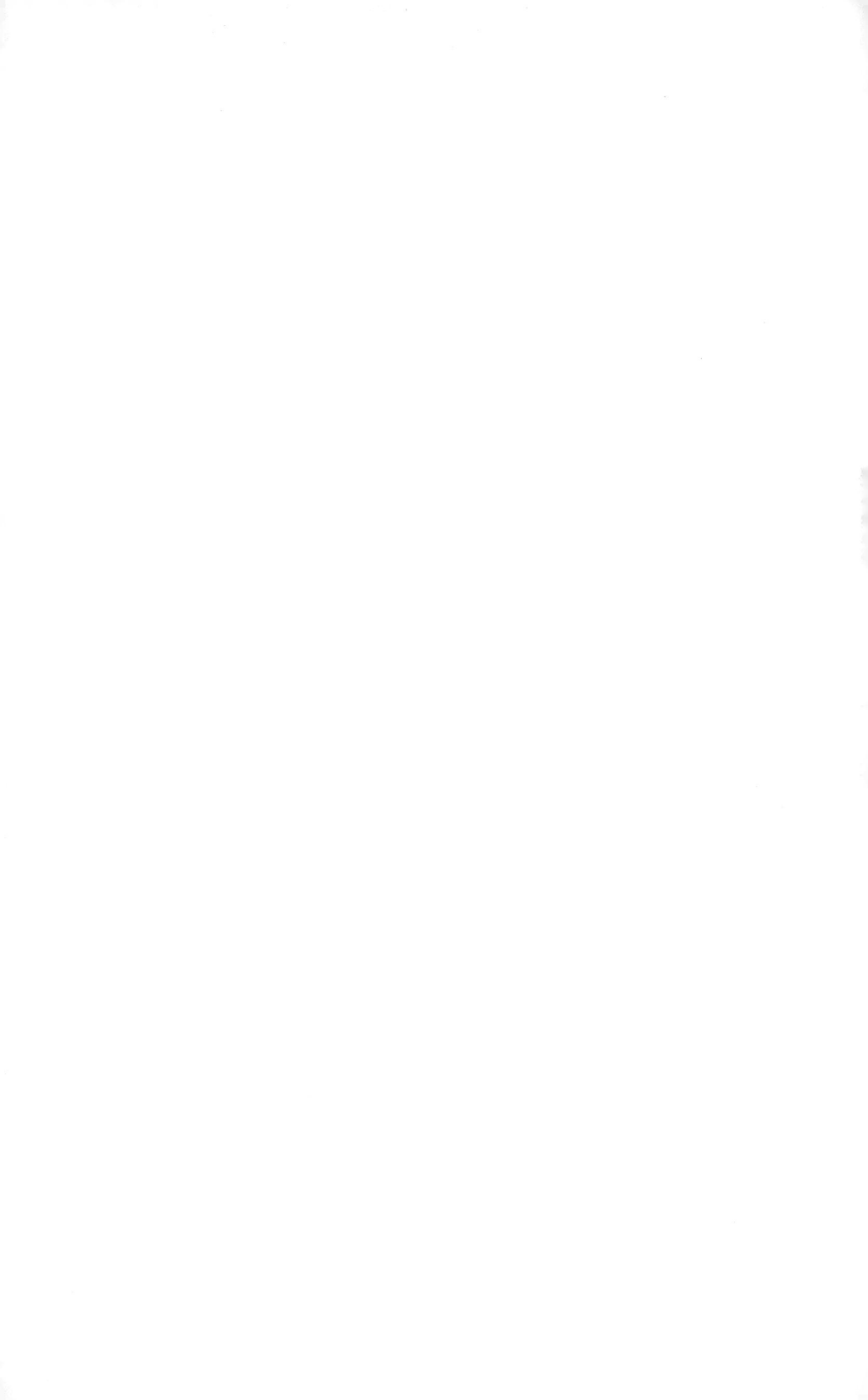

www.ingramcontent.com/pod-product-compliance
Lightning Source LLC
Chambersburg PA
CBHW040812200526
45159CB00022B/485